DAME EVERGREEN

And Other Poems of Myth, Magic, and Madness

REBECCA BUCHANAN

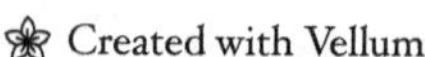

Scream Queen Extraordinaire and completely unbiased friend of the author

Myth, fairy tales, legends, and fables provide rich soil and richer fertilizer for Buchanan's creativity. The poems she has crafted here are stories you may have *thought* you knew, but as you read them, you will find out that there are at least parts of the stories you have never heard of before. Young maidens, old witches, owls, and wolves nestle side by side with each other, all waiting their turns to slip gently into your head and stay there forever. — Jennifer Lawrence, author of *Listening for Their Voices* and *In Their Company*

I remember an age
When the forests were still haunted by holiness
When dryads of mossy hair
barky skin
eyes of tree-shadowed pools
Ran wild
Knit a dance with goat-eyed Pan
When Dionysus offered wine of joy and sadness
to vine-mad maenads
And Artemis braided blood-stained lilies
through her night silk hair
I remember an age
Holy
Haunted
Eternal Summer

— (after Milton)

Contents

Introduction

The world is magic, and the world is poetry, and the ingredients to create new poem-spells — whether as sonnet, sestina, ghazal, or free verse — are as varied as those who cast them.

A sleeping princess. An angry Goddess. A bloody cosmogony. A moss-stained tombstone. An ancient grave. A darkened temple. Historical marginalia. The harsh call of a corvid. A half-remembered dream. A dancer in the window. All of these and more have served as inspiration — ingredients, if you will — for the poems in this collection.

The mythical.

The magical.

And the mad.

Among the Briars

they walk among the roses and thorns,
shadows within the brambles:
their bones gleam by sun and moon:
birds have made nests of their armor,
rusted and cracked open:
whispering warnings unheeded,
they walk among the roses and thorns

shadows within the brambles
they wander, lamenting
lives lost to folly and lust,
ghostly steps silent upon the rot
of leaves and feathers and flesh
as they drift, forlorn,
shadows within the brambles

their bones gleam by sun and moon
and their skulls, still toothed, mock
the foolhardy and the brave alike;
coronets and ruby rings
are treasures for crows and

osseous chimes clack in the breeze as
their bones gleam by sun and moon

birds have made nests of their armor,
stripped bits of moldy fabric and threads
of gold and silver, piled them in gauntlets
still bent to clutch swords long lost;
upturned helmets catch the rain,
becoming pools for mice, snake, and fox, while
birds have made nests of their armor

rusted and cracked open,
breastplates have become home to skulks
of foxes and husks of rabbits, snakes
hunt mice among the vambraces, butterflies
alight on shields once as bright as their wings,
and spiders make traps of chainmail now
rusted and cracked open

whispering warnings unheeded,
they go mad in their anger; spectral
eyes seek out her high tower; a desperate
few claw in futility at the vines and stone,
evaporating in the warmth of the sun,
leaving mad, muttering shades to wander,
whispering warnings unheeded

they walk among the roses and thorns,
shadows within the brambles:
their bones gleam by sun and moon:
birds have made nests of their armor,
rusted and cracked open:
whispering warnings unheeded,
they walk among the roses and thorns

birth

He leans down from the tree, grey
beard stained red, reaching
into the
void
between ice
and fire. Dancing,
they will themselves incarnate.
Hungry, they feast on
blood freely
giv'n.
Sovereign,
they name none master,
not even he who called them.

Bodvild's Lament

my love
my love
my devious love

my father maimed him
my brothers chained him
my mother laughed
and hung the key at her belly

my love
my love
my treacherous love

in secret
my brothers stole into his forge
make us goblets of gold and ivory!
they sang
throwing ash in his face
jewels to be envied!
brooches to rival the moon!

my love
my love
my scheming love

he took their heads
and from their skulls
he forged goblets of gold and ivory
from their eyes
jewels of blue and green
from their teeth
brooches to rival the moon

my love
my love
my traitorous love

the goblets to my father
the jewels to my mother
the brooches to me
and for himself their bones
their blood
their fat
their skin

my love
my love
my deceitful love

he broke his chains
on wings of bone and flesh he took flight
seizing his freedom
forsaking my love
and the son who will be as clever as he

"But he is naked," the child chanted

Glamour shredded,
unwoven,
he stood exposed,
pale in his vanity,
feet bare and bloodied on the stones.

Sated, satisfied,
the tailors slipped into fae,
to the sharp smile of their queen,
needle bright
as she sewed her tattered heart
whole again.

Calchas stands upon the cliffs of Aulis

before him
the ships of Hellas
a thousand strong
lie helpless
sails hunting a still wind

behind him
kings rage

before him
a great eagle
a fish twitching in its grasp
a pair of ravens
circling round and round
a woodpecker
chipping away at the mast of a ship
a sun-blind owl
falling into the sea
a vulture
crooked-necked
swooping down to feast

behind him
kings rage

Calchas stands upon the cliff of Aulis
cursed to know the will
of an angry Goddess
he weeps

cat sí

nine times
a witch may assume
her feline form

the first time
and the second
and on through the eighth
she may resume her womanly shape

not so
the ninth

and so it was
with my mother
fleeing fire and knives
her belly already round

and in the dark of the moon
i was born
quick of mind and clever of tongue

black-furred and black-eared
a white spot upon my heart
where the inquisitor had branded her

Dame Evergreen

Now comes the time of Midwinter's Hag,
when holy sun hides her face, night rules
longest, and stars cut the open sky.

Now comes the time of the Hoarfrost Maid,
when mountains howl and the trees
stand as bare-boned sentinels.

Now comes the time of Dame Evergreen,
who braves hungry snow and cunning ice,
basket of coal and bright torch in hand.

In cloak of red, she walks. Her loyal
page, wrapped deep in furs of wolf and bear,
knows safety in her steps. Basket

of bread and basket of mead held close, he
follows his Dame through the Yuletide night.
Town to town, village to village, door

to door they walk, offering fire

to the cold, light to the lost, food
to the hungry. Now comes the forest

of Midwinter's Hag. Upon her great white
bear she rides, balding and brittle-boned.
"Food, drink," the Hag says, voice the creak

of frozen branches. "I hunger, I thirst."
Red of cloak, Dame Evergreen offers
bread and mead, piece by piece, sip by sip,

until the Hag has filled her gaping
belly, and both baskets hang empty
from the page's trembling hands. Silent,

fiercely grinning, Midwinter's Hag rides
into Yuletide's deepest night. On they
walk, town to town, village to village,

door to door. Now comes the high mountain
of the Hoarfrost Maid. Upon her great
black wolf she rides, hunched and knife-eyed.

"Food, drink," the Maid says, voice the crash of stone.
"I hunger, I thirst." Dame Evergreen,
red-cloaked, offers bread and mead, piece by

piece, sip by sip, until the Hoarfrost
Maid's ravenous belly is full, and
the twin baskets hang hollow from the

page's shaking hands. Laughing, with a
feral smile, the Hoarfrost Maid rides
into Yuletide's darkest night. On they

walk, town to town, village to village,
door to door, Dame Evergreen's bright torch
lighting their way. As the longest night

yields to the day, and holy sun at
last shows her shining face, Dame and page
set aside torch and coal, cloak of red

and coat of fur, baskets now empty
true. In beds of yew and pine they seek
their short rest. Soon will come the time

to sow the seeds, build the nests, and dig
the burrows. Soon will come the time when
the Hoarfrost Maid's voice of stone becomes

the roar of rain-fed mountain streams. Soon will
come the time when the frozen-forest
voice of Midwinter's Hag becomes

the pulse of rich tree sap. The way will be
made. Soon the time when Springtide's Child
and the Vernal Queen waken the world.

Deianaira's Apology

the poets, they called me naïve
my husband
     — ah, the great hero —
he called me tame

blind, all of them
to my woman's rage
a rage I wove
with blood and pain
and set ablaze

Donkeyskin

First, father's favored daughter,
wedded and bedded and runaway.
Now, prince's prize deceived,
her laughter a manic bray.

Do Not Test Your Tongue

by daring to try my names
    (and i have many)
do not dare to twist my names
with tongues foreign and clumsy
say them true

Ahuic
    (parting one and then the other)
    streams splitting and splitting

Apozanolotl
    (white-capped, rich with foam)
    the sea churning and heaving

Atipac Calqui Cihuatl
    (she who lives in the sea)
    throne of coral and bone

Atlacamani
    (storm sea)
    grey-black with rage

Atlacoya
    (sad waters)
    drought, cracked earth, cracked lips

Atlatona
    (she who shines in the waters)
    glittering, dancing, untouchable

Ayauhteotl
    (mist of morning, mist of night)
    hiding mountains, sea, and sun

Ayopechcatl
    (she who dwells on the back of the tortoise)
    hard-shelled, thick-legged, ancient-eyed

Chalchiuhtlicue
    (jade her skirt)
    source of all waters salt, fresh, and brackish

Huixtocihuatl
    (salty, salt-tongued)
    coat your lips, daughters, and dance

Xixiquipilihui
    (wind upon the mountain lake)
    frosted breath, frosted cheeks

say them true
say them true
say them true

doors

one door
appeared in the night
only a few inches tall
and bright red
growing among the roots
of a large oak tree

a mother saw it
jogging in the early fog
her toddler in a stroller
her retriever on a leash

the dog whined
and tried to run

she did not understand

curious
she stopped
fiddled with the latch

the dog
shrieking
lunged on his leash
dragging her across the ground

the toddler
alone
giggled
and wiggled
slipping free of the stroller

the second door
appeared high
in an ash tree
unnoticed
until a cat got stuck

the fireman
who climbed up to retrieve it
found the cat
sniffing curiously
purring
at the bright blue door

the third
so bright a green
that it stung the eyes
hid among the tangled branches
of a stunted hawthorn
growing from a crack
in the pavement
behind an abandoned warehouse

only the squirrels
ever saw that door

it didn't matter

three doors

they only needed one

and a child
laughing
to invite them out
to play

Exhibit #0214269

Item: Human heart

Date: 3rd century CE

Status: Incorruptible

Description: Heart (human, likely male). Odour of Sanctity (often described as a combination of rose, vanilla, sugar, and sometimes cocoa). Myroblysia a.k.a. Oil of Saints (flows only once each year, on 14 February).

Additional Notes: Seek the saint's blessing at your own risk. Museum is not liable for any fatalities, natural or otherwise. Please form a line, single file. No cutting, no shoving, no fighting. Graphomania will manifest suddenly and violently. Sit down or find a wall to lean against as you compose your perfect love letter/poem/song. Pen/pencil and paper are traditional, but not recommended for safety reasons. Tablets and phones are preferable. Perfect love letter/poem/song guaranteed. Happily ever after is not.

Five Suns

to the west, white
to the south, blue
to the east, red
to the north, black

from white blue red black
come rain jade skull flowers stars moon earth
sun

Nahui-Ocelotl
first sun
black
a world of dusk and shadows
white drives black from the sky
with a club of polished stone
chips fall to the earth
angry
black screams a jaguar scream
blind in the darkness
the people are a feast

white blue red black
rain jade skull flowers stars moon
begin again

Nahui-Ehécatl
second sun
white
the people forget
that they are people
enraged
black laughs a monkey laugh
the people grow tails grow fur
flee their houses for the trees
mourning
white takes up his club of polished stone
swings it round and round
a divine wind
to wipe the world clean

white blue red black
rain jade skull flowers stars moon
begin again

Nahui-Quiahuitl
third sun
rain
who loves flowers
who loves black
grieving
rain weeps fire
burns the earth
the people grow feathers grow wings
flee their houses for ashen skies

white blue red black

rain jade skull flowers stars moon
gather the ash
stain their hands lips cheeks
and begin again

Nahui-Atl
fourth sun
jade
who loves the people
and is loved by the people
mocking
black accuses jade
of deceit hypocrisy selfishness
heart-broken
jade weeps blood
drowns the earth
the people grow fins grow scales
flee their houses for pure waters

white blue red black
rain jade skull flowers stars moon
begin again

Nahui-Ollin
fifth sun
blue
rules jaguars monkeys birds fish
heart-broken
white descends to skull's house
and steals the people's bones
consecrates them with his own blood
and the people awaken
again
beneath the bright day sky

Flora Rides the Fifth Avenue Bus

flora rides the fifth avenue bus
her arms are covered in tattoos
thorny wild roses
warm yellow dandelions
proud black-eyed susans
peonies and pansies dance across her collarbones
and bees tickle her throat
lavender and wisteria climb her calves
and
'round her ankles
ivy
visible for only a moment as she skips down the aisle
skirt swirling
and pirouettes out the door

The Frog's Tale

happily is not *ever after*

a frog became a man
for love of a princess
but brought too much
of his frogness with him
the flies
the hopping walk
the long baths
the babes
who would not stay in her belly
and came out crooked and green

he leaves in the night
not even a kiss farewell
while she pretends to sleep
back to the pond
where she had lost
her little golden ball
back to the colony

beneath the lily pads
where tadpoles gather
to hear his tale
and think

it will be different for me

<h1 style="text-align:center">grave-gifts</h1>

a knucklebone
swollen and pitted with arthritis

a blue marble
smooth but for the jagged crack
cleaving one side

a lullaby
a mother never got to sing
to her newborn son

dog tags
dented and scratched

a baby's tooth
uncut

she walks through the cemetery
collecting them one at a time

the knucklebone

rolls to her of its own accord
eager

the marble
is a hard lump beneath her foot
sullen and frightened

she kneels in the wet grass
listening to the lullaby
as she turns the knucklebone and marble
between her fingers

the dog tags
lay just beneath the surface
of fresh-turned soil

she has to dig for the tooth
in an unmarked plot
along the outer fence
while the infant wails incoherently
through his trash bag and rags

the knucklebone
goes to the granddaughter
who treasures the quilts
her grandmother continued to make
even as her fingers bent and twisted

the blue marble
goes to the man
walking through the prison gates
a reminder to hang from his keychain

the lullaby
she writes down in a neat hand

on fine paper
and slips beneath the front door
of the widowed father

the dog tags
she delivers in person
to the legless marine
and then holds him while he weeps

the tooth
she keeps for herself
she fills her pockets with them
strings them around her neck and wrists
tokens of the lost and abandoned
as she walks cemeteries uncounted
gathering the gifts of the dead

gray mare

he came home from the war
and told her a tale
of an iron-gray mare
who led his tank
past metal carcasses
through a field of mines
on a moonless night
and then faded
with the mist of dawn

Her Pearl

Her pearl is caught, is trapped by tide,
by cup of crag. *Too far,*
too far, the mother weeps. Her bairn,
he burns to black and tar.

How to Birth a Witch's Toolbox

Begin with the bones of your foremothers
burnt black
thigh bones are too long
forearms are best
touch them all
choose the one that fits your hand true
whittle the end to a point with sharpened stone
flint or obsidian
wash your wand with dirt from the graves of the lost & forsaken
& blood from coat hangers & bathroom floors

Return to the bones of your foremothers
burnt black
forearms are too short
thigh bones are best
four or six
long & thick
cut off your hair
baring your scalp
take three of your own

& three from your mother
& three from your grandmothers
& three from your great-grandmothers
& twine the bones together
straight & true
braid your shorn hair round the knobby end
adding beads & shiny stones
threading & weaving a fine bristle
for your broom of bone

Return to the bones of your foremothers
burnt black
skulls are best
touch them all
choose the one that fits your hand true
pack the eye sockets with earth & shining stones
the teeth too
cut off the top of the skull
& fill your cauldron with your tears
& those of your sister who cannot speak
& your sister with the hidden bruises & breaks
& your sister with the glass-cut cunt

Finally return to the bones of your foremothers
burnt black
the long finger bones are best
whittled to a point with sharpened stone
flint or obsidian
cut your left eye free
wash it in the dirt of abandoned & forgotten graves
& the blood of child-brides
& the salt water of your cauldron
polish the cornea & sclera 'til they shine
& return it to your skull

& see the pain & anger of your sisters
& take up your sharpened stone
& your wand & your broom & your cauldron of bones
the bones of your foremothers
& whittle the world

How To Build an Altar to the Morrigan

Begin with a feather,
black,
but iridescent,
shimmering purple-blue
when you spin it in the light.

Next, a candle;
white is best,
for bones and teeth and purity.

And a bowl;
for blood,
you may think.

Yes,
but more:
into the bowl
spill your fear,
your anxiety, your bitterness,
memories of betrayal and panic,
the ache of self-loathing.

Sacrifice
your weaknesses,
that which makes you less.

Offer them to Her,
a feast for the Raven
who gorges on dead things
leaving only the vital and the strong.

Hymn to the Headless God

when the monk came scuttling out
white-faced, thin-lipped, agitated,
the lieutenant,
curious,
grabbed a light and a thermos
and started down
into the ancient bowels
of the ancient abbey

i trailed along
more out of boredom
than anything else
down one staircase after another
through narrow passages
strewn with rubble and bones and dirt
knocked loose by a rain of axis bombs

we found it
in the lowest level
in the oldest section
of the abbey cellar

the stone wall
that had hidden it
for millennia
cracked and fallen away

nude
male and female in one
breasts and cock colorfully painted
headless
sword in one hand
cup in the other
headless dog at his-her feet

the lieutenant
a heathen in his heart
laughed
saluted
splashed his coffee on the ground
and ambled away
leaving me to lie to the priest
that no pagan offerings
had sullied his sacred precinct

Hymn to Melinoë

nightmares
live on the bottom of a lake
just south of the fields of asphodel

melinoë
is the only one
who will visit them
she sits on the bank
of that still mercury-colored pool,
tossing in bits of pomegranate
and sometimes mint and saffron seeds
and she watches the waters dip
and burble
for just a moment
as the nightmares fight over the treats
she giggles
sticks her toes in the freezing waters
and whispers to the nightmares
of the treats that await them
in the minds of sleeping mortals

If You Would Seek a Seeress

You will find my grave
before the gates of Hel,
across the bridge of blades,
at the end of the iron road
that bends and twists through the nine worlds
like a sharp-toothed snake.

Bring honey, a black lamb,
a handful of seeds
— any seeds will do —
and an iron wand bound in brass.

When you find my grave
— it will not be marked —
kill the lamb, skin the corpse,
wrap the wand and seeds
in the soft black wool,
dig a hole at my feet,
and place the bundle inside.

Pour the honey,

and call me.

If I am pleased,
or bored,
or curious,
I will come.

Do not run.

Ask your question with respect.
(It must be important to you,
to have taken such a journey
down the iron road.

It is not important to me.)

If I am pleased,
or bored,
or curious,
I may answer.

You may be satisfied
with what I have to say,
or disappointed, or angry.

That is no concern of mine.

I will take the iron wand bound in brass
and the soft black wool and the seeds
and the honey, and return to the
feasting halls of Hel.

I will drink and sing with the dead
as we wait for the wolves
to eat the sun and the moon,

for the nine worlds to succumb to fire and ice,
for the tree to fall at last.

And in the ash
and the mud
and the bones
your seeds will grow.

in the palace of the giant

the stairs are teeth
the walls are stacks of bone
mortared with fat

he hears only the golden song
that called him to climb
the twisting twining vine
climb until his hands bled
and his nose bled
and his ears darkened with frost

he does not hear the scrape
of the mortar and pestle

In the tower I wait

I cut my hair and wove a rope,
a noose to hang a prince.
He mocked my no, my tears;
condemned my love, my witch.

Iphicles, On His Brother's Return

my children see him first
at the rise in the road
and run to him
shrieking and giggling
or gaping in awe
his club is over his shoulder
freshly stained
and the lion skin is around his hips
claws and teeth still sharp
my youngest daughter reaches forward
curious
but he gently takes her hand
before she is cut
and throws her across his shoulder
she kicks and laughs
they're a raucous horde
as they barrel through the door
shouting questions
begging for stories and feats of strength
but he is quiet

my wife shoos and cajoles the children away
she welcomes him with a kiss
standing on her toes
he has to bend down

i see the ghosts in his eyes
the guilt
loneliness
rage
hunger

i take his hand
welcome him home
and
for a time
the ghosts are quiet
and he can rest

Kali Ma, Found Again

It was the heat
that drove her
into the heathen sanctuary,
the blasted Indian sun
that she had so loved as a child,
swimming free in the Ganges.

In the shade of the temple,
sweating through her petticoats
and her tight-boned corset,
she paused,
blinking and panting.
She ripped off her gloves
(a gift from her pale mother-in-law),
and her hat
(foisted upon her by a pale sister-in-law)
pressed her hands and forehead
to the cool stone.

Sweet-scented air filled her lungs,
coated her tongue with the taste of

honey and orange and cinnamon.
One hand to the wall,
she staggered further into the temple,
kicking her skirts out of the way
(another gift, from another pale sister-in-law).

Her eyes cleared
and, from the darkness,
the idol emerged:
black-haired
bright-eyed
red-lipped and gilded
sticky with offerings of orange and milk,
saffron and cinnabar,
honey and wine.

The skirts that she had come to hate
— oh how she hated them —
caught her feet and sent her sprawling
across the cool stones.

Hands raw,
she pulled herself to her knees
and buried her head in her mother's lap,
and wept.

Lament of Echo's Daughters

forgotten,
we seek refuge
in mountain meadows thick
with wildflowers,
calling, calling, calling
mother's name

our own voices
answer

The Library of Trees

books remember

abandoned
the roof falls in
and the walls cave in
and the floor cracks wide

the rain and the sun
touch their spines
and they remember
that they were trees
once
deep rooted and tall

and trees they become again
pages melting beneath water and light
falling
settling in the rich earth

and they grow
trunks engraved with the words

of cather and whitman
leaves shimmering
with the verses of basho and dickinson
branches whispering
whispering

winds rise and rush
storms carry word-seeds
high and far
forests of poem-ash and myth-maples
groves of tragic-oak and satire-thorn
grow deep-rooted and tall
a world of stories
nurtured
by a library of trees

little bears

they wore bear skins
those little girls at Brauron
stamped their feet and growled
growled from deep in their bellies

little girls don't dance as bears anymore
they vomit to stay weak and skinny
wear heels that make them stumble and fall
sculpt and paint their useless nails
hold their tongues and smile and don't growl

little girls aren't bears anymore

little turtle

it's a media circus
helicopters and drones
circle overhead
and traffic is backed up
the roads impassable for fifty miles

the police are overwhelmed
so the national guard
is called in

the little girl
who spotted the turtle
has been on every talk show
and is getting a free ride
to harvard
whether she wants it or not

the pictures are pixelated
but the world upon its back
is clear:
mountains and meadows

rivers and trees
and tiny cities

so is the egg
carefully set in a hole
and covered with sand
before the turtle ambles away
back into the ocean

(the nest site is surrounded
by five layers of armed guards
who shoot down any drone that gets too close
plus three fences
and a hundred or so cameras
that scientists monitor
every second of every day)

there are protestations
of course
that this whole thing must be a hoax

until the egg cracks
and a little turtle emerges
barely the size of that little girl's palm
infant world upon its back
and everyone stops
just stops
and wonders
and wonders
again

Luminescent Giant Butterfly Lady

myself
wings luminous
in the darkness of before

i spread my thighs
breathing the first breath
and birthed sun

too brilliant
i caught him between my wings
took his light
born of my own
sculpted it
into one orb two a hundred a thousand
and cast them out into the darkness

i spread my thighs
breathing the second breath
and birthed serpent
rainbow scales

i caught him between my wings
took his scales
born of my flesh
sculpted them
feathers fish claws teeth
two-legged four-legged no-legged

breathing the third breath
i danced

mama always says

beware the fairy at the well

she changes her shape
wrinkled hag with swollen knuckles and stooped shoulders
fair maid with shining eyes and soft hands

no matter the gift
say no

always say no

or you may end up like me
hiding from greedy kings and princes
spitting diamonds and pearls from bloody gums

Neaera's Complaint

bright and honey-tongued he was
until the girls
golden
popped out of my belly
and he whisked them away
in a whirlwind of fire and light
to an island
on the western edge of the world
with none for comfort but one another

really
i do wonder sometimes
if he knocked me up
just so he'd have someone
to watch his wretched cows

A Plea Whispered Into Dark Waters

I am surrounded by your statues
the little ones that fit in my palm
(when I am allowed to touch them)
and the large ones
so big that I feel I might fit in your mouth
sharp teeth closing round me
dark
quiet
like the bottom of your river

I am afraid

Are you real?

I need you to be real

I hurt
He hurts me
I am afraid

He will be traveling your river tomorrow

carrying all those statues that he has dug up
taking them away to be gawked at in distant museums
taking them from your homeland

All but one
this little one

I managed to keep it hidden
I give it back to you now
Take him
take him down into the quiet of your river
food for your children
take him away from me

Do this thing
and I shall save your statues
as many as I can
set them back upright in the sun
give you good beer and bread
as they did in old days

I am afraid

Crocodile, do you hear me?

Pliny's "How to Perform an Augury"
WITH MARGINALIA BY CATHERINE MONVOISIN

First, divide the heavens into
quarters. Face the north, with the east
to your right and the west on your
left. Stand with your back
to the warm southern breeze.

north is the direction Romulus faced;
equals victory and success; right hand by rising sun
for renewal, rebirth; left is sinister, by setting sun,
death, endings; and the sun is behind
so the birds and their shadows are clear

Next, watch for these birds:
raven, thick-beaked and dark-winged;
woodpecker, with his bright red crest and spotted breast;
owl, moon-eyed and silent on the wind;
eagle, swift and strong;

vulture, curve-beaked and shadow-winged.

raven for healing, illness, cunning, gullibility;
woodpecker for business, building, loss, disaster;
owl for wisdom, ignorance, night, day;
eagle for victory, defeat, strength, weakness;
vulture for death, rebirth, balance

Finally, be still. Breathe. Listen. Open.
Count their numbers. Hear their calls.
Watch them in their flight, and know.

owl, eagle, vulture on the left
they are coming for me

The Pomona of Park Avenue

nude
she stands
above the waters
partly shaded
by branches barren and tangled
cornucopia in one hand
overflowing with apples oranges peaches pears plums
pruning knife in the other
dulled and chipped
but still held high
proudly

coins shine in the water
pennies mostly
a nickel here and there
penurious offerings to a goddess
few can name

the princess dropped her golden ball

down down down it sank
into the green depths

a frog rose in its place
golden-eyed
and promised her treasure
in exchange for a kiss

lips touched cold skin
down down down she sank
shedding her human hide
amphibian princess
once lost
now found again

The Queen and Mistress Kitty

Mistress Kitty, what do you hear?
Shrewd claws, my Queen.

Mistress Kitty, what do you smell?
Sickness, my Queen.

Mistress Kitty, what do you see?
A rat, my Queen.

Beneath your silks, beneath your throne,
a foulness, sharp-toothed and quick.
But quicker am I, keen of ear
and nose, sharper than any rat.

Rightly I Am Called

She came over the mountains
   over the hills
   over the plains
   through forests and valleys
Her long hair dragging behind
   entangling trees
   rocks
   lions
   wolves
Banging her drums
Shaking her bracelets
   her anklets

King of the Gods, he calls himself
   claiming throne and sky
   — he even tried to steal my drums,
   hurling thunder

But Mother of All the Gods am I
My daughters and sons are sky
   and sea and

earth and underearth
Spirits of flame
    and salt water and
    wood and cave

Rightly I am called
Great Queen
Good Goddess
Mother of Mountains

As I dance and
    sing and
    drum

Across the world

roads are the roots of cities

roads are the roots of cities
toxic tar and petroleum
smothering strangling choking

Earth cracked
split the roads
gashed them deep

walk not the roads,
sings the oak

walk not the roads,
sings the ash

walk not the roads,
sings the thorn

they do not listen,
the horned and the hoofed
the furred and the feathered
they do not listen

becoming food for the roads

they loom over the horizon
those hungry cities
with bones of steel and teeth of glass

in the night
their strange lights blot out the moon
frighten owls
confuse bats singing for their prey

in the day
their fumes blot out the sun
poison the rain
turn rivers to acid

roads are the roots of cities
smothering strangling choking
Earth mile by mile by mile

The Skin

She is the seventh daughter
of the seventh daughter
of the same father
who fears the son
who will usurp his throne of golden shit.

He should have feared *her*.

Soldiers salute,
eyes averted,
ashamed.

She slips through the stable door,
sheds her golden crown,
her golden dress,
her golden slippers.

The knife is sharp.
The donkey's skin is hers.

Wet and warm,

she wraps it 'round her swollen belly
and,
barefoot,
is away through the gate,
into the night,
into the woods,
braying her triumph.

The Skull

Skulls surround the house
by the dozens and
the hundreds. Some are
yellowed with age, cracked,
missing teeth. Others

are fresh, meat dangling
like ribbons. They do
not interest her.
The red-haired doll in
her pocket quivers.

She rests a soothing
hand on the poppet's
head, as her mother
had once done for her.
The chicken claws scratch

at the ground. The skulls
watch, jaws gaping. The
door creaks open and

Grandmother is there,
and her smile is

hungry, and she holds
a staff, and a skull
sits atop that staff,
eyes burning, red hair
dangling like ribbons.

Sleeping Beauty's Lament

I dream of briars, bones, and blood.
The dead, entangled, rage.
A kiss to break the curse. A lie.
Awake, I dream, encaged.

steadfast

he is watching me
through the window
across the street
ratty ribbons and dull medals
hang from his dirty green jacket
the crutch buys him sympathetic coins
i can hear the mad rattle
as he shakes his little tin cup
demanding that i see him

my smile is for the girls
as i lead them across the bright floor
which smells of warm wood and lemon
dancing
to the soft swells of bizet
they make silly faces and giggle at their reflections

trapped
between window and mirror

he is watching me

a stranger in the cemetery whispered
to me

it is said by those
who claim to know the
truth of such things that
only two-legged
animals possess
souls. perhaps this is
the way of things. i
tell you this, though: bright-
eyed raccoons and great-
antlered stags haunt the
edges of every
road, spirit flocks of
geese make their way from
winter land to warm
land and back again,
and a quiet snake,
shadow-scaled, rests in
the roots of a long
dead oak tree. i have
seen no two-legged
ghosts.

the tales of corvids

corvids are collectors
you know
baubles and bits
and shiny things
that match the gleam
of their ebony eyes

they collect other things
too
stories mostly

owls may be wise
but it's corvids who know
the tales of old

they remember
the towers of glass and steel
and the noisy canyons of rushing wind
and the tiny patches of green
where people would throw them
bits of bread and bits of beads

they remember
when the people went away
and the rushing winds
and the reborn rivers
began to wear away at the glass and steel

they made nests inside those crumbling towers
pulled threads and buttons and cufflinks
and built treasure piles for themselves
and their greedy chicks

and told them tales
of the noisy world
now grown quiet and green

turtle

she didn't tell anyone
not a single soul
of what she saw on the beach that night

the great turtle
as big as a house
emerging from the ocean
a world upon its back
mountains and rivers and trees and meadows
and tiny tiny cities

the turtle looked at her for a long moment
neck stretching
and then began to dig
slowly
feet scraping in the sand

she got on her knees
to help
pulling out armfuls of dirt

the egg dropped into the hole
a glossy gleaming white

the turtle kicked the sand back over it
looked at her again for another long moment
and slipped back into the water

she sat there through the night
shooing away crabs and hungry seagulls
until
at last
the sky a pale blue-grey
the little turtle
barely the size of her palm
clawed its way to the surface
infant world upon its back
clouds drifting
among tiny mountains
rivers rolling
into tiny lakes

lifting its head
the turtle sniffed
following the scent and sound of water

the tide threatened
to shove it back onto the shore

she caught it carefully
holding it steady
fingers brushing the back of its shell

she followed it awkwardly
arm stretched out
sand sinking beneath her knees

the water rising
rising
to wet her chin

with a last kick
the turtle was gone

she tasted salt
uncertain
if it was the sea
or her tears

(untitled)

poor girl
from a poor village
in a poor country
long enslaved
raised on stories of Chava
and Sarah and Hagar
and Keturah and Rivkah
and Leah and Rachel
and Zilpah and Bilhah and Dinah
and Tamar and Asenath
and Yocheved and Miryam
and Elisheba and Tziporah
and Rachav and Devorah and Yael
and Huldah and Naomi and Rut
and Chaanach and Bat-Sheba
and Abigayil and Michal and Yehudit
and Hadassah and Shoshannah
heard God in a garden

and said *yes*

Welcome to the Library

My doors are always open
I don't mind if you're a bit grubby
(I do like the smell of trees)
But please wipe your feet

My caretakers are sharp-eyed
and sharp-tongued
Speak politely
and never lie

I have lots of comfortable chairs
If you fall asleep
best to do it in the mathematics section
The fantasy books always need new heroes
and the mysteries always need new victims

If you pack a lunch
be sure to bring enough to share
The dragons sunning in the windows
enjoy a good French cheese
and the cats

slipping among the shadows
are particularly fond of asparagus

Children are encouraged
to laugh and dance and play
The books will come out to watch
Don't worry about putting them back
They know their way home
Keep watch though
as they may try to take
some of their favorite children with them

Treat my books gently
I will know if you do not
So will my caretakers
When they ask how this page was torn
or that spine was broken
do not lie
for it is not only
the dragons and the cats
who are hungry

Wish

Basile. Perrault.
The Grimm boys,
with their heavy sideburns.
The author is irrelevant:
in every version, it is all about *her*.

The fairy,
owl-eyed,
did not have the heart
to tell the soot-covered girl,
that she was there for the rat.

A Witch, Hunting

I wear my daughter's cloak
the hem shredded
when she tried to run.

Her blood is a splash
of darker red
against the crimson cloth.

Don't leave the path.

I walked that path,
as did my mother
and her mother before her
and her mother yet before her
on back through the years
a red thread
tying us together.

Don't stray off the path.

A simple rite for a dark moon,

not easy
— it is not meant to be easy —
but she knew the way
and she knew the words.

And yet
come the dawn
there was only her cloak
and her blood
and a single wolf's print.

I wear her cloak now,
the hood torn
when she tried to run.

Knife in hand,
the moon dark in the sky,
I step off the path
— and the red thread breaks.

Worthy

the magic is all for them
always for them
it has to be saved
hoarded
for those deemed worthy

never me

dishes pile high
caked with the grit of
dinners consumed and forgotten

laundry spills out of baskets
all over the floor
wrinkles and stains and what
is that brown smear?
do i want to know?

push the squeaky cart
up and down
up and down

aisle 1 2 3 4
how many aisles are there?
where's the damn cheese?

advertising
gods how i hate advertising
post here
post there
like this back
like that back
network network network
read *all* the emails

because one
maybe two
but probably only one
will be *the one*
worthy
of all my damn dirty dishes

Author's Notes and Comments

Among the Briars — inspired by the classic fairy tale "The Sleeping Beauty."

birth — a poetic imagining of the discovery of the runes, based on Norse lore.

Bodvild's Lament — in Germanic lore, Bodvild is a tragic and complicated figure. Her exact relationship with Wayland the Smith evolves through the myth, and is open to a variety of interpretations.

"But he is naked," the child chanted — inspired by Hans Christian Andersen's "The Emperor's New Clothes."

Calchas stands upon the cliffs of Aulis — in the lost epic *Cypria*, the famed augur Calchas declares that Artemis will not allow the Greek ships to sail for Troy until her anger is appeased through the sacrifice of Iphigeneia.

Dame Evergreen — a mash-up of the Triple Goddess with the Christian folktale of King Wenceslaus.

Deianaira's Apology — in Greek polytheism, Deianeira is one of the many wives of Herakles; and the one who ultimately kills him (accidentally?).

Donkeyskin — inspired by the classic fairy tale of the same name.

Do Not Test Your Tongue — Chalchiuhtlicue, with her many names, is the Aztec/Mexica goddess of water, rivers, seas, streams, storms, and baptism.

doors — be careful.

Exhibit #0214269 — inspired by the legend of Saint Valentine.

Five Suns — in Aztec cosmology, a different God rules each cardinal direction. These Gods, in turn, created the other Deities, and went on to create each of the five worlds (or suns). Each world/sun was destroyed in succession. We live in the Fifth Sun, which, it is prophesied, will end in earthquakes.

Flora Rides the Fifth Avenue Bus — Flora is the Roman Goddess of flowers, and is celebrated in the annual Floralia.

The Frog's Tale — inspired by the classic fairy tale "The Frog Prince."

grave-gifts — an original poem inspired by the cemetery near my home.

gray mare — Epona is the Central European/Roman Goddess of soldiers, cavalry, and horses. Some modern polytheists honor her, by extension, as the Goddess of tanks and other mobile warfare.

Her Pearl — inspired by mermaid lore, and tales of pearls as mermaid eggs.

How to Birth a Witch's Toolbox — inspired by the deaths of all the witches who have come before.

How to Build an Altar to the Morrigan — The Morrigan is the Celtic Goddess of war, fate, doom, death, strength, guardianship, sovereignty, and victory.

Hymn to the Headless God — inspired by tales of the Monuments Men during the Second World War.

Hymn to Melinoë — Melinoë is the chthonic Goddess of nightmares and madness in Greek lore.

If You Would Seek a Seeress — inspired by the recent discovery of a burial in Northern Europe of a sorceress/runeworker.

in the palace of the giant — inspired by the classic fairy tale "Jack and the Beanstalk."

In the tower I wait — inspired by the classic fairy tale "Rapunzel."

Iphicles, On His Brother's Return — according to Greek lore, Iphicles is the mortal half-brother of Herakles.

Kali Ma, Found Again — Kali Ma is a much-love Hindu Goddess who was widely misunderstood by European colonizers.

Lament of Echo's Daughters — in Greek polytheism, Echo is a nymph who pines away for love of Narcissus and becomes nothing but ... well ....

little bears — inspired by a traditional rite in ancient Athens in which girls, prior to the onset of puberty, were sent to the sanctuary of Brauron; there, they honored the Goddess Artemis in a variety of rites, including dancing while dressed as bears.

little turtle — inspired by a half-remembered dream.

Luminescent Giant Butterfly Lady — Mu Olokukurtlisop is the Creatrix in the spiritual tradition of the Cuna people of Panama.

mama always says — inspired by the classic fairy tale "Toads and Diamonds."

Neaera's Complaint — in Greek lore, Neaera bears two daughters, Phaethusa and Lampetia, by the Sun God Helios; they protect his sacred herd of cattle on the island of Thrinacia, as discovered by Odysseus and his crew in *The Odyssey*.

A Plea Whispered Into Dark Waters — in ancient Egyptian polytheism (modern Kemeticism), Sobek is a protective, if ruthless, crocodile Deity.

Pliny's "How to Perform an Augury" with Marginalia by Catherine Monvoisin — Gaius Plinius Secundus was an ancient Roman author, naturalist, and naval/army commander; sadly, most of his writings have been lost. Catherine Monvoisin, also known as La Voisin, was the head of a large network of fortune tellers in Paris; charged with fortune telling, sorcery, and poisoning, she was burned to death on 22 February 1680.

The Pomona of Park Avenue — in Roman polytheism, Pomona is the Goddess of apple trees specifically, and fruit trees and orchards more broadly.

the princess dropped her golden ball — inspired by the fairy tale "The Frog Prince."

The Queen and Mistress Kitty — inspired by the classic nursery rhyme "Pussy Cat, Pussy Cat."

Rightly I Am Called — in ancient Greek polytheism, Rhea-Kybele is the Mother of the Gods. She is closely associated with mountains, lions, caves, and drums.

The Skin — inspired by the classic fairy tale "Donkeyskin."

The Skull — inspired by Russian tales of Baba Yaga.

Sleeping Beauty's Lament — inspired by the classic fairy tale "The Sleeping Beauty."

steadfast — inspired by the Hans Christian Andersen fairy tale, "The Steadfast Tin Soldier."

a stranger in the cemetery whispered to me — another original poem inspired by the cemetery near my home.

turtle — inspired by a half-remembered dream.

(untitled) — in Catholic theology, the Virgin Mary is the mother of God Incarnate.

Welcome to the Library — because every good poetry collection should have at least one poem about the magic of libraries.

Wish — inspired by the classic fairy tale "Cinderella."

A Witch, Hunting — inspired by the classic fairy tale "Red Riding Hood."

Worthy — surely the fairy godmothers must have something to say.

Publication Credits

[Author's Note: by-and-large, the poems appear here as originally published. However, like many writers, I continue to fiddle. Astute readers may notice some differences between the poems here contained, and how they originally appeared.]

Among the Briars — original version published in *Quantum Fairy Tales* (Winter 2016)

birth — *The Diviner's Handbook: Writings on Ancient and Modern Divination Practices* (Bibliotheca Alexandrina)

"But he is naked," the child chanted — *Enchanted Conversation* (August 2017)

Calchas stands upon the cliffs of Aulis — *The Diviner's Handbook: Writings on Ancient and Modern Divination Practices* (Bibliotheca Alexandrina)

Dame Evergreen — *Faerie Magazine* (Winter 2016) [Rhysling Award nominee 2017]

Exhibit #0214269 — *Riddled With Arrows* 5:1

Five Suns — *The Far-Shining One: A Devotional to the Spirits of the Sun* (Bibliotheca Alexandrina)

Flora Rides the Fifth Avenue Bus — *MOON Magazine* (March 2015)

grave-gifts — *Polu Texni* (July 2017)

gray mare — *The Grey Mare on the Hill: A Devotional Anthology* (Grey Mare Books)

How to Birth a Witch's Toolbox — *Three Drops From a Cauldron: Full Moon and Foxglove* (October 2016)

How to Build an Altar to the Morrigan — *By Blood, Bone, and Blade: A Tribute to the Morrigan* (Bibliotheca Alexandrina)

Hymn to Melinoë — *The Dark Ones: Tales and Poems of the Shadow Gods* (Bibliotheca Alexandrina)

in the palace of the giant — *Star*Line* 40:2 (Spring 2017)

Iphicles, On His Brother's Return — *The Dark Ones: Tales and Poems of the Shadow Gods* (Bibliotheca Alexandrina)

If You Would Seek a Seeress — *Star*Line* 41:1 (Spring 2018)

The Library of Trees — *Polu Texni* (August 2018)

little bears — *Unbound: A Devotional Anthology for Artemis* (Bibliotheca Alexandrina)

Luminescent Giant Butterfly Lady — *Garland of the Goddess: Tales and Poems of the Feminine Divine* (Bibliotheca Alexandrina)

mama always says — *Gingerbread House* (Winter 2017)

Neaera's Complaint — *Call of the God: An Anthology Exploring the Divine Masculine Within Modern Paganism*

Pliny's "How to Perform an Augury," With Margunalia by Catherine Monvoisin {originally published as "How to Perform an Augury"] — *The Diviner's Handbook: Writings on Ancient and Modern Divination Practices* (Bibliotheca Alexandrina)

Rightly I Am Called — *MOON Magazine* (March 2015)

Sleeping Beauty's Lament — *dreams&nightmares* 124 (May 2023)

steadfast — *Enchanted Conversation* (March 2017)

a stranger in the cemetery whispered to me — *Eye to the Telescope* 22 (October 2016)

the tales of corvids — *Abyss and Apex* 3:18

(untitled) — *Dappled Things* (Spring 2011)

Wish — *Gingerbread House* (March 2015) [Dwarf Star nominee 2016]

All other works are original to this publication. Copyright Rebecca Buchanan 2018, 2023, 2024.

About the Author

REBECCA BUCHANAN
PAGAN FAERIE TALES · FANTASY · ROMANCE

Rebecca Buchanan is the editor of the Pagan literary ezine *Eternal Haunted Summer*. She has published multiple short stories, novelettes, and novellas, which she is in the process of collecting, as well as two poetry collections, with more on the way. A complete list of her publications may be found on *Eternal Haunted Summer*.

Novellas and Novelettes
The Adventure of the Faerie Coffin:
Being the First Morstan and Holmes Occult Detection
Asphalt Gods:
A Walking the Worlds Adventure
Geek Witch and the Treacherous Tome of Deadly Danger:
A Tale of Magical Dice, Cursed Books, and Blackberry Jam
The Maiden and the Marrow Witch:
A Tale of Magic and Murder
The Secret of the Sunken Temple

Poetry
Dame Evergreen, and Other Poems of Myth, Magic, and
Madness

Not a Princess, But (Yes) There Was a Pea, And Other Fairy
Tales to Foment Revolution (Jackanapes Press)

Forthcoming
The Ballad of the Chalice and the Blade:
A Tale of Friederich the Bard
Blood, Honey, Snow:
A Tale of Murder at the Edge of the World
The Bones Are Walking, And Other Pagan Urban Fantasy Tales
Eleanor Tilney and the Black Dog of Beechen Cliff:
A Hidden Regency Adventure
Grandmother Granddaughter Wolf, And Other Poems Fae,
Fearful, and Fantastic
Jane Fairfax and the Siren of Weymouth:
A Hidden Regency Adventure
Malkin:
A Tale of Magic, Espionage, and Too-Curious Cats
Rueppelli and Yerik in the Great Bazaar of Repet-Yark:
A Walking the Worlds Adventure
Vesta's Fire:
A Tale of Roma Aeterna